Living Your DREAM

The UNREAL DEAL

by Suzanne Weyn
illustrated by Ben Shannon

by Michael Leviton

GLOBE FEARON
Pearson Learning Group

CONTENTS

The UNREAL DEAL

How to Rock

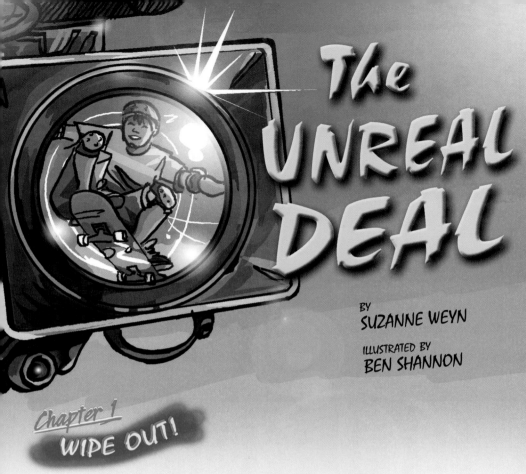

The UNREAL DEAL

BY
SUZANNE WEYN

ILLUSTRATED BY
BEN SHANNON

Chapter 1
WIPE OUT!

Carlos stepped onto his skateboard, unsteadily balancing at the top of the ramp. He anxiously looked over his shoulder and spotted Alicia Keane. She was still casually glancing his way as she chatted with two of her girlfriends.

He'd never expected her to show up at the skate park today. She had **probably** been to the dance squad tryouts being held at the community center next to the skate park. It was an unbelievable stroke of luck. This was his moment to impress her with his skateboarding expertise.

With a last darting glance at Alicia, Carlos pushed off and zoomed down the U-shaped ramp. He had the bottom of the ramp in sight, preparing to skate up the opposite side. That's when a dark **distortion** darted toward him.

A black cat scampered across the bottom of the ramp!

"No!" he shouted, swerving to avoid the animal.

The cat screeched to a halt as the skateboard flew out from under Carlos's feet and continued on up the ramp without him.

He soared into the air!

Thwap! The bottom strap of his left kneepad snapped loose just before he slammed onto the ramp.

His left knee, the one with the loose pad, screamed with pain as he skidded across the cement. The impact, coupled with his wild slide, scraped open his jeans and his skin. He let out a howl in pain before remembering that Alicia was watching.

For a split second, he hoped that she'd race to his side, alarmed and concerned about his injury, and offering him help. When she didn't appear, he quickly faced the truth. She'd witnessed his total **humiliation**. In all **probability**, she now believed that he was a complete loser.

"Hey, man, you okay?" asked another skater as he descended the ramp. "That knee looks nasty."

Carlos forced himself to stand, wincing as he straightened his leg. "Stupid cat got in my way," he grumbled. Shifting his eyes toward Alicia and her friends, he watched them climb into a car that drove off.

Carlos retrieved his board and limped toward his house, which was four blocks from the skate park. When he got there, his older brother Sam's car was the only one in the driveway.

He went into the kitchen, pulled a paper towel off the roll, and dampened it at the sink. Dropping down into a kitchen chair, Carlos began to dab his injured knee with the soggy towel, carefully clearing away dirt and tiny debris embedded in his skin.

"Hold it right there!" Sam swept into the kitchen, the family video camera held to his eye. "This is just what my film needs, real-life drama! Tell us, Carlos, in your own words, how this hideous injury occurred."

Carlos ducked his head and waved Sam away. "It's none of your business. Why don't you get lost?" he snapped irritably.

"That's where you are wrong!" Sam insisted, focusing in on Carlos's bloody, scraped knee. "All of America wants to know how you came by this obviously horrific injury. Was it a daring act that spiraled out of control, revealing the dark side of bravado and resulting in stunning **humiliation**?"

Carlos blinked at him. "Well...yes...in a way," he admitted. "How did you know?"

"Cut!" Sam shouted. He straightened and turned off the camera. "Now, you might nod in **agreement**, that's great film making," he praised himself cheerfully.

"How did you know what happened to me?" Carlos asked again. He needed to be assured that the whole town wasn't gossiping about how he'd wiped out in front of one of the cutest, most popular girls at school.

"No big deal," Sam assured him. "You were **probably** showing off for some girl, right?" Carlos nodded glumly. Sam patted him on the back, making him less sad. "That's how these things always happen," he added confidently. "Your worries are over from now on, though. You are about to become the most popular kid in town."

Carlos looked up at his brother with a skeptical expression. Sam had always been a little "out there," but now it sounded as if he'd finally flipped. "What are you talking about?" he asked Sam.

"You've heard about that new show, _American Ideal_, right?" Sam asked. Carlos had seen ads for the upcoming **reality** TV show. It was going to feature real families and events that represent ideals in American life.

"I'm entering a video of our family," Sam explained. "If we get picked, our family will represent the ideal American family."

Carlos snorted with distaste. "_This_ family? Are you kidding?"

"No joke," Sam assured him. "I think we really have a chance!"

"What's in it for you?" Carlos asked, knowing his brother wouldn't do this unless it would benefit him.

"I just want America to appreciate how awesome our family is," Sam insisted.

Carlos fixed his brother in a doubtful stare. "That's nice," he said. "Now give me an answer I can believe."

"All right, you're onto me," Sam said with a shrug. "I figured it would be a good way to get my band on TV."

Now *that* was an explanation Carlos could believe. Sam was the lead singer in a garage rock band, Green Eggs and Sam, and had been trying to get the band on TV. They performed in the rain at Town Day, hungry for any free TV airtime. The cable channel never aired the program.

After that the band wore comical glasses and entered a funniest home video contest sponsored by another TV show. They didn't win. They didn't even get on the show.

Obviously, this videotape was the latest of Sam's schemes to get Green Eggs and Sam TV airtime. "Everyone will see us perform on *American Ideal*," Sam explained. "We'll be famous."

"Famous?" Carlos questioned. "Totally **humiliated** is what we'll be."

By the following Friday, Carlos had stopped worrying about having his family featured on *American Ideal*. Thousands of families had undoubtedly entered. Carlos figured that the **probability** of his family's being picked ranged from slim to none.

There was one thing, however, that was still distressing him. Alicia Keane used to glance his way occasionally and honor him with a quick half-smile if she passed him in the school hallway. Now, she completely ignored him.

In the days that followed his skating disaster, he'd attempted to catch Alicia's eye and speak to her about it. He'd even developed a collection of witty remarks that would indicate to her that he thought the whole thing was extremely funny, just a big joke. "I guess you saw me do my airborne cat trick," was one of his favorite prepared comments.

If she inquired about his knee, he'd pretend that he didn't even remember hurting himself. "Oh, that," he imagined saying dismissively. "Skateboarders get banged up like that all the time."

Day after day he'd hover near her locker. There was no need for him to be there. He'd just pretend to be doing something extremely important, like tying his shoe or stuffing a note in someone's locker.

"When are you going to give it up?" asked his friend, Rae, one day while Carlos was loitering near Alicia's locker. Carlos had been pretending to study a flier announcing the next Chess Club tournament.

"I don't know what you mean," he insisted.

Rae laughed. "Yeah, like you're really **intrigued** with that Chess Club information," she scoffed. They'd been friends since kindergarten and she understood him better than anyone else. She knew all about his crush on Alicia.

"I figure she'll **probably** forget all about the skateboard thing pretty soon," he said hopefully.

"You can think that way if you want, but it's not likely," Rae disagreed. "Once you've **humiliated** yourself in front of the popular kids at this school, you're off their list. You might as well be invisible."

"Thanks a lot, Rae," he chided her.

"Sorry," she replied with a shrug of her shoulders. "I'm only trying to be **realistic**. Just forget about her. There are a lot of other girls in school who are just as pretty and much nicer."

"There is no one else like Alicia," he argued. "I'm going to ask her to the dance at the end of the month."

Rae sputtered, as if this news had caused her real physical discomfort. "You're crazy, Carlos! What world do you live in?"

"I live in the real world, same as you," he insisted. "I just feel that eventually I can get Alicia to like me. *You* like me, *don't* you?"

"Of course I like you," she replied. "You're a great friend, but that's different."

He suddenly stopped and stared down the hall. Alicia was coming toward him, her arms piled high with books.

She hesitated in front of the water fountain. Shifting her books from one arm to the other and back again, she attempted to activate the water button. She was too bogged down with books, however, to manage the task successfully.

Once again, an unbelievable chance had presented itself to him. He couldn't believe his luck!

Determined to seize this opportunity, he rushed over to the water fountain. "Allow me," he offered, trying to sound smooth, like an **intriguing** and polished man of mystery.

Just as she turned toward the fountain, Carlos pressed the metal button. A stream of water shot into the air, much higher than he had expected.

It hit Alicia directly in the eye!

"Aaahh!" she screamed, squinting and dropping her books as she jumped back. "You idiot!" she yelled.

While Carlos stood in shock, Rae grabbed his arm to pull him down the hall. "I can't believe I did that," he said, shaken by this mishap.

"Face it," she said. "Be **realistic** and admit you can't win with her."

"Maybe," he said, but deep down he wasn't convinced. He was still pondering new ways to win over Alicia when he arrived home. Walking into the kitchen, he saw that the message light on the answering machine was blinking.

Had Alicia called? Did she want to apologize for being so short tempered? He couldn't really blame her, though. After all, he had squirted her in the eye.

Intrigued, he pressed the button on the machine. Instead of Alicia's voice, a man spoke. "Hello, this is Robbie McMyers, director of *American Ideal*."

Carlos could hardly believe it! He grabbed a pen and jotted down the telephone number. After dialing and getting Robbie McMyers on the phone, he listened carefully.

"We have good news," said Robbie. "Your family has been chosen to be televised. Your submission was approved by our background checkers. We start filming right away."

10

"Don't throw those away!" Carlos told the man from *American Ideal* who was tossing boxes of cereal into a large trash bag. "Those are my favorites!"

"The ideal American family does not eat this stuff," the man explained as he ripped open a large cardboard carton. He pulled out boxes of new, different cereal. He began replacing the old cereal with these new boxes. "*This* is what they eat."

"Why?" Carlos asked.

"We promised the show's sponsors that our ideal Americans would only use their products," the man explained. "The sponsors pay for the TV **commercials**, which is how we earn the money to put the show on the air. Get it?"

"I get it," Carlos told him. "I thought this was supposed to be reality TV, though."

"It may be real, but it's still TV," the man commented as he went to check that they had the proper products in their freezer.

Carlos walked into the living room where all around him the producers, directors, and crew members of *American Ideal* were scurrying around **transforming** his home. They claimed it was too packed with furniture, leaving no room for the production crew, so half of what his family owned was now banished to the garage.

They said the walls were too dull, so painters were busy slathering them in a vivid blue color. Even the dog, Lola, was thought drab. She was given a doggie T-shirt to wear that said "Rock on!"

Carlos's mother came down the stairs, and he saw that she, also, had been **transformed**. Instead of the usual jeans and T-shirt that she wore on weekends when she wasn't at work, she had on a black leather skirt, sunglasses, and lace-up black boots.

"I didn't know you even owned a leather skirt," he remarked, looking shocked.

"Oh, this thing? I've had this packed away for years," she said while smoothing out the leather. "Robbie said I'd seem more supportive of my children if I showed my interest in their music."

"But you already are supportive," Carlos reminded her.

"That's true," she agreed, "but Robbie thought I should have a definite contemporary look." From the corner of the room, Lola began clawing at her doggie T-shirt. Mrs. Cruz hurried off, in her clicking boots, to stop Lola from ruining the shirt.

Carlos scratched his head. Things had sure gotten crazy in the last three days since his family had been selected to be featured on *American Ideal*.

The high-pitched whine of an electric guitar blasted from the family room. Sam leapt into the living room, clutching his guitar. He'd shaped his hair into small spikes and had thrown a cape over his usual clothes. "Rock 'n' roll!" he shouted.

A tall man with a ponytail motioned to Sam from his wheelchair. The man reached up and fixed Sam's cape collar so that it stood straight up. Carlos thought it made Sam look like Dracula, but Robbie McMyers seemed pleased with the effect. "Now you look like a real rock 'n' roller," he remarked.

Carlos's dad came into the living room and draped his arm over Carlos's shoulder. "Don't you think this is a great opportunity?" he asked.

"Is it?" Carlos questioned.

"You bet," his dad assured him. "I plan to take advantage of freebies. I just mention a product's name on the air and the company sends it. It's like a free **commercial** for them."

Giving Carlos a hearty slap on the back, his dad made his way over to talk to the show's director. Carlos shook his head with a feeling of pity. Even his sensible dad had caught the **reality** TV fever.

Carlos glanced out the window and his heart sped up. Alicia was on the sidewalk in front of his house along with four other girls. They were **probably** curious to discover what the *American Ideal* TV trucks were doing in the driveway.

Maybe she'd think he was cool because he was going to be on TV. He could go out and tell her! He was on his way when an anxiety-producing thought hit him. All of America— and Alicia—would see how weirdly his family was behaving! He'd be publicly **humiliated**!

"Hey, Carlos," said a man in his twenties who'd come up the front walkway. "I see the **reality** TV gig is in full swing."

"Tell me about it," Carlos replied to his Uncle Ricky. Glancing over Uncle Ricky's shoulder, he saw Alicia and her friends walk away. At least it was one less thing to worry about.

Thank goodness his uncle had come by. At least one normal family member would be around. "It's like a circus in there," Carlos commented.

"I love the circus," Uncle Ricky commented, clicking his heels together in the air.

Carlos frowned. Maybe Uncle Ricky wasn't quite as normal as Carlos had thought.

By the time Carlos arrived at school on Monday, everyone there seemed to know *American Ideal* was filming at his house. He hadn't told anyone but Rae, so he could only assume that Alicia and her friends had hurried away and done their own version of Paul Revere's ride. The only difference being that instead of alerting everyone that the British were coming, they'd notified the population that *American Ideal* had come to the Cruz's home.

"I'd like to interview you for the school paper," said the paper's editor, Freddy Hinckle, holding a pen and notepad. "What is it *really* like having *American Ideal* in your life twenty-four, seven?"

"Believe me," Carlos told him, "you don't want to know." Carlos's first thought was to reply with "**disastrous**." How could he explain that his life had been **transformed** from its usual state?

Carlos now had an annoying but manageable series of **humiliating** moments all adding up to one big nightmare. What words could convey the horror of living in a home now completely **overcrowded** with camera crews, production crews, and makeup and lighting people? Robbie McMyers and the camera crew even camped out overnight in their family room.

Perhaps the hardest thing to explain would be the effect that being on the show had on his family. How could he possibly describe to Freddy the **transformation** that had come about ever since the show had actually started filming late Saturday afternoon?

His mom was determined to present herself to the TV audience as a cool rock 'n' roll mother. She never took off her sunglasses and now had somehow acquired a pink streak in her hair.

His father had become a walking **commercial**. He mentioned a new product in every breath, hoping to get as much free stuff as possible.

Sam was the worst. He never just stood or sat anymore. Now he only moved from one rock-star pose to another.

"Freddy, I really can't find the words to describe it," Carlos said. "You'll just have to see it for yourself when it comes on TV."

"When will that be, Carlos?" Freddy asked.

"In a few months, I guess," Carlos replied. He knew it would be a summer show. At least he wouldn't be in school when it aired. He could hide in his room all summer if he had to.

"Thank you, sir, for your…umm…personal thoughts," Freddy said as he hurried off toward the editorial room to file his report.

Alicia and two of her friends walked by. "Hi, Carlos," they said simultaneously, smiling sweetly at him.

Stunned, Carlos simply stared at them. It occurred to him that wild animals that had been shot with tranquilizer pellets probably felt the same way he did—panicked and paralyzed at the same time. He needed a **reality** check. It didn't seem possible, and yet, it had happened. Perhaps this whole *American Ideal* thing wouldn't be completely **disastrous**.

He'd apparently become a celebrity in school, and that seemed to impress Alicia. He considered the fact that it also meant she didn't sincerely like him for his true self. However, he hoped that would change once she got to know him.

At least she wouldn't see his bizarre family on the show until *after* the dance. Alicia wouldn't know he was going to be humiliated in front of the entire nation until she'd already gone to the dance with him. By then, she'd be completely in love with him and wouldn't care.

Carlos walked home that afternoon with a spring in his step. Things were looking up!

His bouncy stride froze in midstep, however, when he saw what was happening on his front lawn.

A circus from the Shakespearian era had sprung up on his lawn.

15

Acrobats jumped, rolled, and stood on one another's shoulders while a man juggled pins and minstrels strolled by strumming on lutes. The *American Ideal* camera crew filmed it all.

Uncle Ricky met Carlos on the lawn. "Hail, young nephew," he said with a theatrical flourish of his hand. "Recall thee that I told thee I joined an experimental company of thespians that uses acrobatics and dance in their Shakespearian plays?"

"I guess so," Carlos replied. He didn't really recall this, but he knew Uncle Ricky was an actor.

"I admit that with us here it's a little **overcrowded**, but alas! We hath lost our rehearsal space," Uncle Ricky went on, dropping his Elizabethan gestures and accent. "Your father said I could bring the acting company here as long as we mentioned products whenever we're on camera."

Robbie McMyers joined them. "This is great TV!" he said excitedly. "I'm going to ask the network if we can air some of it before the summer schedule. America's got to see it now!"

Carlos sat in bed thinking about what Robbie McMyers had said. He wanted to air the show—or at least some of it—before the summer schedule. Uncle Ricky was elated at this news, but Carlos could not share his **enthusiasm**.

If that show went on before summer, all the kids at school would get a good look at the lunacy and **chaos** going on in his family. He'd never live it down and, what was worse, Alicia would never, ever agree to go to the dance with him.

Sam jumped into his room, twirling his cape. "Which pose is better?" he asked. He sucked in his cheeks and lifted his cape up to his chin. Then he switched positions, throwing the cape back over his shoulders and standing with his hands on his hips.

"I don't know," Carlos replied. "The first pose makes you look like Dracula and the second one makes it seem as if you think you're Superman."

"I'll use the first one then," Sam decided. "It fits my image better."

"Why do you need a pose, anyway?" Carlos asked.

"Robbie just told us some good news," Sam answered. "His network said they can't air the show before the summer."

"That *is* good news," Carlos said **enthusiastically**.

Sam looked at him as though he were strange. "*That's not the good news*," he said. "The good news is that Robbie is going to put together some film footage and show it at the end of his other reality TV show, *Bachelor Survivors*. I love that show. It's about guys who avoid getting married."

A sickening lump formed in Carlos's stomach while panicked thoughts whirled **chaotically** in his brain.

There was only one thing to do—they'd have to move! That would do no good, though. *American Ideal* would air across the nation. Everywhere he went, he'd be laughed at. All across America everyone would know him as the kid with the goofy family.

Canada might be the answer. No, they'd probably see it there, too. Did they get American TV in Europe? He didn't know—maybe they'd have to go farther than that. "Do they watch American TV in China?" he asked Sam.

"I hope so," Sam replied. "I've always wanted to be an international superstar." With a dramatic swirl of his cape, Sam galloped out of the room, leaving Carlos alone with his stomachache and his desperate thoughts.

For the next few days, Carlos did nothing else but wonder what film footage Robbie would use for the *American Ideal* "Sneak Peek." He hoped it wouldn't be anything too **humiliating**. Alicia kept on smiling at him, but he couldn't work up the nerve to actually speak to her.

"This is your big chance to ask Alicia to the dance," Rae reminded him. "She'll want to show up with a TV star as her date."

"If I ask her now she might say yes, but she'll **probably** just dump me once she sees that 'Sneak Peek' at the end of *Bachelor Survivors* next week," Carlos said.

"I bet it won't be as embarrassing as you think," Rae suggested hopefully.

"You're right," Carlos agreed. "It'll **probably** be worse."

Carlos returned to the **chaos** of his home each day. As his mother tripped over Lola while trying to prevent the dog from tearing the T-shirt with its teeth, Carlos turned red over the entire event. He was so embarrassed that he wished he could simply disappear.

When Uncle Ricky and his acting troupe recited Shakespeare's lines as they did front and back flips and mentioned products, Carlos cringed. He was imagining how it was going to look on TV.

Worse than this picture was the thought of Alicia seeing it! He enjoyed having her smile at him. That would change forever once she saw how ridiculous his family appeared on TV.

"It's official!" Robbie McMyers announced on
Wednesday afternoon. "We've put together some really
dynamic footage to show at the end of *Bachelor Survivors*,"
he told the family, crew members, and acting troupe that had
assembled around him. "I only need five more minutes of
footage and it's ready to go. I need something really exciting
or hilarious to hook the viewers."

Carlos knew what Robbie really meant. He wanted a
piece of film that was so ridiculous and embarrassing that it
would make viewers scream with laughter. He couldn't just
wait around for Alicia to see this humiliating event on TV.

Then, suddenly, he knew what he needed to do. It was a
wild plan, but right then, he felt completely desperate. It
would have to be done that very night.

Chapter 6
HUNG UP

This was going to be tricky. Sneaking past the camera crew on his way out of the house wouldn't be easy. Even in the middle of the night, one of them was always stationed on the couch with a camera, watching for any footsteps or movement. The night before, the cameraperson had followed him all the way to the bathroom, waited at the door, and then followed him back to his bedroom at three in the morning.

Carlos, making a break for it, went out onto the deck above the family's attached garage and quietly climbed down the back steps. Soon he was standing in his dark backyard. Secretly he scurried down his driveway and headed toward Alicia's house.

If everything went well, it should be fairly simple to keep Alicia from watching him on TV tomorrow night. He would have to locate the cable at the back of her house and disconnect it from the line leading to the transmitter box at the top of the house. Without the cable connection, the cable channels wouldn't play and the network channels would be fuzzy and **distorted**. After the "Sneak Peek" had aired on *Bachelor Survivors*, Carlos would return and re-attach the cable. Alicia's family would **probably** never know why their TV wasn't working for a day.

The lights at Alicia's house weren't on except for the front lamppost. He hurried down her driveway, keeping to the darkest, most shadowy parts.

Carlos reminded himself that he wasn't hurting anything. It wouldn't harm anyone not to watch TV for a night—almost anyone would be in **agreement** with that.

He reached the backyard, bumping into Alicia's brother's trampoline. He dug in his pocket for the small penlight he used for camping. Sneaking around the back wall, he searched for a wire.

There it was!

He'd spotted the place where he needed to disconnect the cable! However, it was connected at a spot higher than he could reach.

As he checked around for a ladder, he became aware of a sound. A light breeze was causing a high tree next to the house to tap a second-story window. Looking up, he saw that one of the tree's branches would lead him right to the cable wire.

Carlos climbed up and was quickly out onto the branch. The leaves shook as he shimmied out, closer to the cable.

Clutching the branch with one hand, he reached out for the small, metal cable connector. It was difficult to unscrew it using only one hand. Inching farther out on the branch, he held on with his knees while he reached forward with both hands.

Carlos squeezed his eyes shut against a blinding light that abruptly lit up everything around him. The surprise threw him off balance. He clutched at the branch and managed to grab hold as his body swung off of it.

Robbie was below, aiming a floodlight at him. He was accompanied by a cameraman. Despite Carlos's stealth, they'd managed to follow him!

Carlos glanced nervously at the windows of the house. Any second, Alicia might appear, awakened by this light. "Turn that off!" he hissed as he began pulling himself back onto the branch.

"This is terrific!" Robbie said, with the light still on him.

Crack! The branch snapped and was hanging together by shards of splintered wood. A cry for help nearly escaped from Carlos, but he clamped down on it. The last thing on Earth he wanted was for Alicia and her family to awaken and discover him dangling from the tree branch in their yard. Could anything be more embarrassing, more totally mortifying and **humiliating**?

On the other hand, if this branch broke, he might not have to worry about anything at all—ever again!

"A little help here!" he called softly to Robbie and the cameraman. He couldn't believe they were still filming while he was dangling high in the air. What kind of **distorted** view of reality did they have? Couldn't they see he was in real danger?

"Oh, yes. Right," Robbie said. He propped the light on a patio table so that it still shined on Carlos. "Keep filming," he told the cameraman, who lowered the camera a moment to nod in **agreement**.

Pete the cameraman put down his camera and dragged the trampoline in from the yard. He positioned it under the tree just as the branch cracked completely in two and Carlos plummeted down! He bounced several times before he was able to control his motion enough to stop.

Breathless, he glanced around. No lights had come on in the house. He was unharmed. Everything was pretty much okay—except that the cameraman was filming him again!

"You're not planning to use this in your 'Sneak Peek,' are you?" he asked Robbie.

"I'm not positive," Robbie replied. "This does seem to be exactly the kind of thing I've been hoping for, though."

Carlos felt positive that Robbie would use the film he'd shot. From Robbie's **distorted** point of view, nothing could be more perfect than seeing a member of his *American Ideal* family looking foolish. The only thing that would stop him was if a bigger catastrophe happened to a member of the Cruz family.

"Are you all set to see the 'Sneak Peek' tonight?" Rae asked him as they walked to class together.

"No," Carlos replied glumly. "I haven't finished digging the hole I plan to crawl into after it airs."

Rae pushed his arm lightly. "You worry too much," she said. "It's very **glamorous** to be on TV. You'll probably be the most popular kid in school by tomorrow."

He hadn't even told Rae about what had happened at Alicia's house, even though he usually told her everything. It was just too humiliating to talk about.

"Hi, Carlos," Alicia greeted him with a smile.

Carlos stopped **abruptly**, leaving Rae to walk on down the hall alone. "Hi, Alicia," he replied nervously.

"I saw a **commercial** about your show yesterday afternoon," she said. "I can't wait to see it come on after *Bachelor Survivors*. I'm sleeping over my friend Mandy's house tonight, and we're watching it together."

"Oh...great," Carlos said, feeling sick. It wouldn't even matter now whether her TV reception worked or not. The tone for the beginning of class sounded, and she hurried away, leaving Carlos even more upset than before.

As he neared his home after school, he was relieved to see that Uncle Ricky and his acting troupe weren't out on the lawn. That was one less embarrassment.

As he got closer though, he saw people on the deck. The high-pitched whine of an amplifier immediately told him who was up there—Green Eggs and Sam.

Thwang! One of the guitarists hit a note that reverberated throughout the neighborhood. A woman with a camera mounted on her shoulder came running out the front door, aiming her camera up at the band. Carlos shook his head and smiled to himself. At least Sam was getting what he wanted out of this deal. With any luck, he'd soon be on his way to seeing his dream of becoming a **glamorous** rock star come true.

Green Eggs and Sam launched into the first of their original hard-rock songs. Carlos stood on the lawn to watch them. Before long, he was joined by a slowly growing crowd of teenage passersby who were attracted by the blasting music. There was some **distortion** and the sound was nearly deafening, and Carlos hoped no one would complain to the police.

After three songs, Carlos's lawn was actually **overcrowded** with spectators. Carlos sniffed the air and smelled something strange. Was there a fire somewhere nearby?

His brother's band caught his attention again. Sam was putting on a real show, twirling his cape, leaping in the air as he sang. They had bigger amplifiers than ever before and more of them. They'd even brought in a fog machine.

Carlos wondered how they'd plugged it all in. He knew there was only one outlet nearby.

Then, he noticed a brown outlet extender with six plug outlets plugged into one receptacle. Plugged into the outlet extender were three more outlet extenders. A jumble of wires all met at the extenders.

He sniffed the air again and that was when he realized what was happening. The band hadn't brought in a fog machine! That wasn't fog—it was smoke!

Carlos's dad suddenly sprang out of the back door onto the deck. He lunged at the outlet extenders, and **abruptly** yanked them all out of the main plug on the wall.

As soon as the music stopped it was replaced with the sound of screaming sirens from fire trucks. The hook-and-ladder truck raced into the driveway.

Firefighters jumped out, attached a hose, and sprayed a powerful jet of foam at the deck. Other firefighters evacuated people from the front lawn.

The camerawoman filmed it all. Carlos saw Robbie rubbing his hands together gleefully. "This is terrific!" he shouted.

Mrs. Cruz ran out of the house with Lola in her arms. She was followed by the other members of the TV crew. Carlos saw that the band and his dad had all made it safely onto the front lawn.

Realizing that everyone was safe and the fire was out, Carlos sneaked a smile as he watched the camerawoman continue to film the smoke and chaos. If there was still time, this disaster might just replace his embarrassing tree episode on tonight's "Sneak Peek" of American Ideal.

That night, the Cruz family gathered around the TV set in their motel room. The smell of smoke in their home was still too strong for them to stay there.

Mr. and Mrs. Cruz, Sam, Lola, and Carlos had all piled onto the same king-sized bed and were watching *Bachelor Survivors*, waiting for the "Sneak Peek" of *American Ideal* to come on at the end. "This show is ridiculous," Mrs. Cruz remarked. "Why would this young man **deliberately** avoid marrying such a beautiful girl?"

"That's the whole concept of the show," Sam told her.

"Quiet," Mr. Cruz snapped at him. The fact that Sam had nearly incinerated the house had made him quite unpopular with his father that evening.

The other king-sized bed next to the one on which they sat held the three members of the TV camera crew who had come to the motel with them to continue filming.

"Our ideal family is stranded in a motel—what great drama!" Robbie had told the camerapeople **enthusiastically**. "Stay on them every second." Then, he wheeled off to edit his "Sneak Peek" film footage.

"After these **commercials** we'll be back with a special 'Sneak Peek' at the new summer show that has everyone talking, *American Ideal*!" the TV announcer said as *Bachelor Survivors* ended.

"Do you think everyone is really talking about this show?" Mrs. Cruz asked, her voice filled with **uncertainty**.

"They will be, after tonight," Carlos mumbled.

The "Sneak Peek" began and the whole family watched attentively. It began with Mr. Cruz facing the camera and saying, "There's no better lawn tractor than the GrassGrabber!"

Next, they showed Mrs. Cruz dancing **enthusiastically** to the radio. That scene led into one with Uncle Ricky and his acrobatic Shakespearians.

Uncle Ricky, wearing a large Elizabethan feathered hat, spoke to the TV screen and told all about the acting company.

"He really looks great on TV. He has such charisma!" the camerawoman commented. "Where is Ricky tonight?"

"The whole group is getting together at the theater to watch," Mrs. Cruz told her.

"Why don't they show my band?" Sam complained.

"Quiet!" said Mr. Cruz.

Carlos was too tense to say anything. Would they use the scene of him in Alicia's backyard?

The screen became very dark and Carlos knew the answer. He grabbed a pillow and buried his head in it, but then he felt forced to steal a glance.

The **disastrous** band performance hadn't replaced his film footage after all!

Though the scene was dark, it was not dark enough. He watched himself fall out of the tree and bounce off the trampoline. He heard a loud ripping sound and, for a moment, he thought he'd torn the trampoline. Then, he saw what had actually happened. He had split the back of his pants without realizing it! The bright white of his underwear gleamed in the moonlight. The cameraman had **deliberately** zoomed in to show it, too.

Carlos put the pillow back over his head. The whole thing was beyond **humiliating**. It was almost more than he could bear!

"Carlos, when did this happen?" his mom asked.

"Uh...the other night," he admitted.

"It **probably** had something to do with a girl, right?" Sam guessed. "These kinds of **disasters** always do."

"Quiet!" Mr. Cruz snapped at Sam.

The family's attention was swept back to the TV by the wail of an electric guitar. Green Eggs and Sam appeared on the screen. "All right!" Sam cheered. They played only a moment of music before the camera zoomed in on the smoking porch outlet.

The family was silent for a moment after it ended. Finally, Mr. Cruz spoke. "I wonder how soon my GrassGrabber lawn tractor will arrive," he said.

"They only showed three lines of my song," Sam complained. "I hope a big producer saw it."

"Carlos, why were you out alone in the middle of the night?" Mrs. Cruz asked.

Carlos thought fast. "I wasn't alone. Robbie and Pete the cameraman were with me. Robbie thought it would make great TV for the 'Sneak Peek.'" It was partly true.

His mom scowled and studied him with **uncertainty**. "Hmm...well...don't do it again."

"Believe me, I won't," he promised, meaning it.

The next morning, Carlos awoke dreading that he had to go to school. He tried coughing and implying that he was suffering from smoke inhalation. When he realized that the camera crew would just film him all day long, he decided it would be better to simply go to school and face the ridicule.

The moment he entered school, the first person he met was Alicia. She stood by the front door with her arms folded. "Carlos Cruz, I've been waiting for you," she said sternly.

Chapter 9
THE UNREAL DEAL

"I was trying to disconnect your cable wires so you wouldn't see the 'Sneak Peek,'" Carlos admitted. "I'm sorry."

"Sorry?" Alicia cried. "If I'd known you were out there, I would have come to the window and then...I could have helped you."

"You're not angry?" he asked.

"Angry? I'm touched that you cared that much about my opinion," she said **enthusiastically**. "How much longer is the film crew going to be there?"

"I think they'll probably be around for another four weeks," he told her. "I don't know how I'm going to last that long."

"Would it help if I came over to keep you company?" she offered.

Carlos suddenly worried that this was a dream, and he wasn't there in school at all. Alicia Keane had just offered to come to his house to keep him company!

"The *American Ideal* people have sent over a crew to clean up from the fire," he told her. "We're moving back in tomorrow. Why don't you come over in the afternoon after school?"

"Great!" she agreed. "Come on, I'll walk to your locker with you." As he walked to his locker with one of the prettiest, most popular girls in school, Carlos was more convinced than ever that he was still dreaming. Adding to the feeling of **uncertainty** was the fact that along the way kids he didn't even know were smiling and nodding at him.

"Funny stuff last night, man," said a boy, giving him a thumbs-up sign.

The rest of the day brought an endless stream of compliments. Everyone seemed to think that Carlos **deliberately** planned his actions. They thought *American Ideal* was to be a funny **reality** TV comedy.

"Alicia is sure intrigued with you now that she knows you were hanging in a tree around her house in the middle of the night with a cameraperson and a director," Rae said to him later that day. "Did you ask her to the dance yet?"

"When she comes over tomorrow, I'll ask her."

When the time came for Alicia to visit, Carlos waited near the curb for her with a cameraperson hovering nearby. Alicia's father's car pulled into the driveway, and Carlos helped her out.

She had changed, though. Her hair looked as though it had been professionally styled. She wore big earrings and a **glamorous**, sparkly dress.

Alicia joined Carlos near the steps but, instead of taking a seat, addressed all her words to the cameraperson. "I am Carlos's gal pal Alicia Keane. I'm an aspiring actress. I'm currently looking for roles that showcase my acting talent while also pursuing a recording contract," she said while flicking her hair back. "My mother, Heather Keane, is my agent and she can be reached at the following number..."

After reciting the telephone number twice, Alicia used the last four digits of the number to finger tap an imaginary rhythm only she could hear. Then, with the same hand, she punched the air and **abruptly** burst into song, Celine Dion-style. Carlos walked away, but Alicia didn't seem to notice.

Four weeks later, Carlos headed out the door to go to the dance. He and Rae had decided to go together, just as friends. From the moment he realized that Alicia was only using him to get on TV, she was no longer the girl of his dreams. He began to think of her as more of a nightmare.

He came downstairs and found the various crews packing up to leave. His mom was once again wearing jeans and a T-shirt. Lola was busy chewing on a jester's hat. His dad checked a list of products to make sure he'd mentioned everything he hoped would be sent to them once the show aired. Sam was on the phone with a record company discussing his upcoming deal.

Uncle Ricky came in to talk to Robbie. "Hey, looking sharp, Carlos," he said. "You got a date?"

"I'm going to a dance with a girl, but she's just a friend," Carlos told him.

"A friend is a great thing to be," Uncle Ricky said. "Have you seen Robbie? I have to talk to him about the new show."

He looked around the busy room and found Robbie talking to a makeup person. The network had received a lot of fan mail for Ricky, so Robbie was now planning a new **reality** TV show about Uncle Ricky and his acting troupe entitled *Shakespeare's in the House*. Robbie waved to Carlos and Uncle Ricky as he came over to join them.

Carlos checked his watch. He didn't want to keep Rae waiting. Through all this craziness, she was the only one who had simply remained herself.

"So long," Robbie said as Carlos waved and headed for the door. "Keep cool. It's been real."

Carlos waved to him and laughed quietly to himself. It had been **chaotic**, crazy, and even kind of fun—but one thing it had *not* been was real!

How to Rock

BY MICHAEL LEVITON

CHAPTER 1
MEET THE BAND

What's your favorite kind of music? Maybe you like hip-hop music. Perhaps you prefer rock and roll. No matter what kind of music you like, you may wonder how your favorite bands achieved success. Although every band's story is different, there are experiences that all bands share on their way to fame and fortune.

My name is Michael Leviton and I'm in a rock band called La Laque. We're not a world-famous rock band—at least not yet. I'd like to tell you about how we started our band and how anyone can start a band.

Of course, not all bands become famous. In fact, most of them don't. Still, being in a band can be a lot of fun, and that alone makes it worth doing. Your band might be asked to play at a local club or at friends' parties. It could be that your band just hangs out and plays in your garage. As long as the members of your band have fun—with the music and with each other— you can consider your band a success.

I'd like to introduce you to the members of La Laque. I am Michael, the electric guitar player. I started playing the guitar when I was 14. I mainly played an acoustic guitar. That was until I tried out my friend's electric guitar. After that experience, there was no going back. I definitely wanted to play loud music.

Devery is our lead singer. "I'm the one everybody looks at, so I **pose** and dance and go crazy on stage," she says. "I'm good at that because I'm an actress." Devery wasn't always comfortable onstage, though. "In middle school, I was shy," says Devery. "But now, I stand on stage in front of everyone and have a great time."

Our drummer is Pete. "Playing drums is more fun than playing any other instrument," he says. "I think I have the most fun in the band." By his own admission, Pete was anything but cool before he started playing the drums. "When I was younger, bullies used to beat me up all the time," Pete says. "Now, I have muscles from playing the drums!"

Brad is our bass player. Brad used to play bass for a jazz band, and sometimes you can hear the jazz influence in his bass playing. "Pete and I establish the beat. If we're playing in front of a lively crowd, they usually **cooperate** and dance to the beat," he says.

Leah plays the organ. A lot of bands don't have organ players, so Leah helps give our band a unique sound. Leah also sings backup vocals, singing with Devery. "Sometimes Devery and I **harmonize**. Sometimes we sing in **unison**," Leah says. Leah's talents don't stop there. "I'm also the band's illustrator, so I make all the posters. I painted the giant *L* on our drums," she says.

Erin also helps give La Laque a unique sound. She plays the violin. Erin's story differs from the other band members' because her background is classical music. For years, Erin dreamed of playing in an orchestra. "I've played classical music my whole life. But I've turned into a rocker."

Meet the band! Seated, from left, are Devery, Pete, and Erin. Standing, from left, are Leah, Brad, and Michael.

Chapter 2
Getting the Rock Rolling

Now that you have met the members of the band, you may be wondering how we came together to form La Laque. It happened almost by chance. It was not a **calculated** decision at all. One day, Devery came to me for guitar lessons. She wasn't much of a guitar player, but she had an **exquisite** voice! We quickly became friends. Then, we started writing songs and performing them together. I played the guitar and she sang. The next thing we knew, some of our friends wanted to join us.

The first time we practiced together was amazing. I think we all knew right away that it was the beginning of something special. "Before that first practice, I thought being in a band was something only other people did," Devery says. "After that, I knew I was born to be a lead singer." Brad adds, "The first time I played with La Laque, it was the loudest I've ever played in my life," he says. "And then they asked me to turn it up!"

One of the best things about the early days of La Laque was coming up with a unique sound for the band. We all had ideas of what our band should sound like based on our musical tastes. Everyone in our band had a different favorite band. Although we wanted our sound to be influenced by the music we love, we wanted to make sure we didn't sound like any other band. How would our music be different from the music of other bands? It's something that really **tormented** us back then.

What kind of unique sound did we create? I've always loved the scary music from old horror movies. We began to experiment with this sound. At first, we just played our instruments. Then, Devery began to sing lyrics. The result sounded scary and dangerous, like a horror movie, but her **exquisite** singing made it different. We had never heard anything quite like it. It took time, but one by one, each member of La Laque fell in love with our sound.

CREATING AN IMAGE

Another thing that is important is a band's image. Some people might say that the only thing that matters about a band is its music. While it may be true that fans like a band mostly for the sound of its music, people also care about a band's image. One part of a band's image is the way it looks. Another part of a band's image is the way it acts on stage. After all, if image wasn't important at all, then why would so many people go to see bands perform live?

Concerts give music fans an opportunity to see how their favorite bands look and act while they are performing their music. For example, Jimi Hendrix was a wild-looking guitarist in the 1960s. He also had a wild sound. Nobody had ever heard a guitar sound the way his did! In concert, Jimi Hendrix played his guitar with his *teeth*! His wild look and wild sound made Jimi Hendrix a must-see performer in the 1960s.

So what kind of image does La Laque have? It's not something that was **accidental**. We took our cue from the music we play. The old horror movies were made in black and white.

When we **pose** for pictures, we all dress in black and white. We wear the same kinds of clothes when we play live shows, so our look is **calculated**. "When everyone in a band dresses the same, it looks like a team," Leah says. "It's great to see a live band that really looks like a band!"

Pete, the drummer, smiles for the camera.

WHAT'S IN A NAME?

Choosing a name for a band is a big decision. You want to pick the best name possible. You can get to the point that almost every name you think of sounds wrong. Think of the names of your favorite bands. Are they any good? If your friend asked, "Should I call my band Radiohead?" what would you tell him? What if your friend said she wanted to call her band Limp Bizkit? Both of these names are kind of strange, but that strangeness can make a good band name. People remember them.

When we were naming our band the decision **tormented** us. We wanted to get it right. We deliberately chose a name in a language other than English. We didn't think a foreign name would be a **barrier**. We thought it would get people's attention. So, we picked *La Laque*. The name rhymes with "rock." I don't remember who first came up with the name. It means "hairspray" in French. If we named our band Hairspray, that would probably sound silly. We thought La Laque sounded a lot cooler.

READY TO ROCK?

Of course, the most important part of being in a band is having good songs to play. After all, you can have the coolest-looking band with the best name, but if the music isn't good, nobody will follow the band. There is no right or wrong way to write songs. Some musicians write the lyrics first and then try singing them. Some bands start playing and a song just happens, almost by **accident**.

In our band, I write the music for the songs by myself. I work on them at home, playing the guitar and humming along until I find a catchy melody. Then, I call Devery and she comes over to learn the tune. Next, she writes lyrics, that is, the words that fit the melody I was humming. After we have the melody and the lyrics, Devery and I teach the song to the rest of the band.

After the band has learned the song, the next step is to practice. Practice is key because bands that make a lot of mistakes don't have a lot of fans. With enough practice, the band will be able to play the songs in **unison** without thinking too much. It's important to know your songs really well. Then, you are able to relax and enjoy yourself when you are onstage.

There are lots of different places to practice. If a band is quiet, it can practice in a house or an apartment. If a band is loud, neighbors will probably complain about the noise. Some towns have buildings with practice rooms. It's important to be **industrious** about finding the right practice space. If you can't find somewhere to practice, it's hard for the band to improve. You need time to learn new songs *and* practice playing the old ones.

La Laque rents practice space in a building full of practice rooms that are just for bands. We share the room with three other bands. The money we earn by playing shows is enough to cover the cost of renting the room.

La Laque practices for 2 hours a day, at least 3 times a week.

38

GETTING ALONG

As you can probably tell by now, the people in a band spend a lot of time together. So band members need to get along. If they fight a lot, the band will probably break up. Breakups happen all the time. In fact, most bands break up after only a few years.

Being in a band is like being in a serious relationship. In a relationship, communication is extremely important. The same can be said about the **management** of a band.

Everyone in a band needs to communicate with each other. If someone is not happy about something, he or she should talk about it with the rest of the band. Even so, there will be **conflicts**. People will fight, and feelings will get hurt. The thing to do when a problem comes up is to talk about it.

It is no **accident** that the musicians in bands that stick together for a long time are very good friends. For instance, the Rolling Stones formed in 1962. After performing with Mick Jagger for forty years, band member Keith Richards said about Jagger in a 2002 interview, "It [the friendship] is a very deep one.... He is a brother."

Sometimes it gets to a point where the only thing left to do is to ask someone to leave the band. That happened once with La Laque, when we had one more singer than we do now. The situation **tormented** everyone involved.

Other than that, we've been pretty lucky. The fact that the members of La Laque are such good friends has helped a lot. Sometimes we get mad at each other, but we are always able to work things out by talking to each other.

CHAPTER 3

BAND BUSINESS

Once you have a name for your band and some great songs that you have practiced over and over again, you're ready to play a live show. In the beginning, it can be hard to convince someone to let you play a show. It takes a lot of patience and hard work to get someone to give your band a chance. Be **industrious**. It's important to never, ever give up. It can take years for a band to become successful.

Most new bands start by playing shows at parties and small clubs. The person in charge of deciding who can play a show at a club is called a booker. A booker usually won't hire a band without hearing some of the band's music. Bookers want to know that the people who come to the club will like the band.

So how can you persuade a booker to hire your band? You need to assemble a "press kit." A press kit includes a bio, a demo, photographs, and a cover letter.

The goal of a press kit is to quickly tell a booker what your band is all about. A good press kit will help your band get hired to play shows in small clubs. It should cover everything there is to know about the band. It should explain the band's music, look, history, and why the band is different from other bands. The press kit should make anyone who looks at it want to listen to the band play.

Creating a press kit for your band is just part of the business of being in a band. Some bands hire **managers** to create press kits for them and to try to get them hired for live shows. Hiring a manager lets the musicians concentrate on the music. However, **managers** are too expensive for most new bands, so the band members have to deal with the business side of being in a band.

Testing, 1, 2, 3. Devery and Leah check a recording.

THE DEMO

The most important part of a press kit is the band's "demo." Demos are rough recordings of songs and usually include two selections. They don't have to be **exquisite**; they just have to give the booker an idea of what the band sounds like. The demo should **lure** the booker into reading the press kit.

There are lots of ways to record demos. Some bands go into a recording studio, but studios are expensive. They can cost anywhere between $50 and $150 an hour. Studios usually have the best recording equipment available. You can adjust the volume on each instrument and the vocals to get everything just the way you want it. If you can pay for studio time, you will get a quality demo. The problem is that the band has to record each song many times to get it right. It can be stressful to record in a studio because every time you make a mistake, it costs money.

Another way to record a demo is to do it yourself. You need a special recorder called an 8-track, or a recording program on a computer. The main advantage to recording your own demo is being able to record over and over for free. That can be fun and also good practice for the band.

WHO ARE YOU?

The next most important part of a press kit is the band's "bio" (*bio* is short for *biography*). A bio is a paragraph that describes the band. A band needs to spend time making sure it gets the bio right. The bio should talk about how long the band has been together. It should include how many people are in the band and the instruments that the band members play. It should also include a phone number or an e-mail address so a booker for a club can get in touch with the band.

The bio has to describe, in an **animated** way, what the band sounds like. The bio should highlight what is unique about your music in a way that will make someone want to listen to your band. For example, you could write, "We have a good beat," *or* you could write instead, "Our beat will bring you to your feet!" Use words that will help bring your bio to life. Just be sure to cover some basic questions. Are you loud or soft? What is the singer's voice like? Are the songs sad? Happy? Scary?

Here's what La Laque's bio says:

"La Laque is a loud six-piece rock band (guitar, bass, drums, organ, violin, and vocals) with whispery girl singers. The band formed in September of 2003 in New York. La Laque mixes wild rock-and-roll energy with organ and violin straight off the soundtrack of an old horror movie. La Laque's mysterious and beautiful front-woman, Devery, sings in whispers like she's about to kiss you…or kill you! La Laque has played at many New York clubs and has shared the stage with New York's hottest bands. Call us at 1-212-555-5555."

As you can see, our bio describes how many people are in the band, the instruments we play, and how a booker can contact us. At the same time, our bio tries to explain what our sound is all about. Getting the bio right can really help sell a band.

SMILE FOR THE CAMERA

The demo and the bio are the most important parts of the press kit. However, it's hard for a booker to get a sense of a band's personality without seeing photographs. It's important to include a couple of photographs of the band in the press kit. Remember what I said earlier: a band's image can be very important. For example, a booker may receive our press kit and think, "La Laque's got a cool sound, but I wonder what they look like." A photograph may **lure** the booker into hiring us.

A band's photographs need to be good, but they don't have to be expensive. There are lots of ways to take pictures for your press kit. Some bands use live pictures of them performing or at practice, while other bands use pictures of the band members relaxing.

Personally, I like band pictures that are taken in interesting places with band members doing **animated** things. These photographs grab your attention. Once I saw a band picture that was taken at an abandoned amusement park. The band was standing in front of an old, broken-down roller coaster. The photograph made the band look really cool! I once saw a band picture where the band was sitting in a diner drinking from a milkshake with four straws, one for each band member. The photograph made the band look fun and romantic.

Luckily, the band members of La Laque love **posing** for pictures. We like our photographs to tell stories; we want them to look like still shots from old movies. Once we took pictures of the band sitting on motorcycles. Another time we took a picture that made it look like Devery and Leah were in a fight. I held Devery back and Brad held Leah back. They both pretended they were really mad at each other! To this day, that photograph is always included in our press kit. Taking pictures like that is fun and can really help your band get noticed.

ARE YOU COVERED?

As you may have figured out, trying to get a chance to play live is a lot like applying for a job. When you apply for a job, you give the employer a cover letter to introduce yourself and a résumé, which shows your experience and qualifications. Your press kit is like your résumé. It shows the booker who you are, what you sound like, and what you look like. The only thing missing now is a cover letter. In your cover letter, you should introduce your band.

Your cover letter needs to communicate to the booker why he or she should hire your band. The goal is to get the booker's attention. In the cover letter, you write a catchy sentence or two that introduces your band. Then, you ask the booker if you can play a show at his or her club. Keep in mind that the reason the club wants bands to play there is to **lure** a big crowd. You should tell the booker how many fans your band can bring to the club. If you promise to bring a lot of fans, the booker will pay more attention.

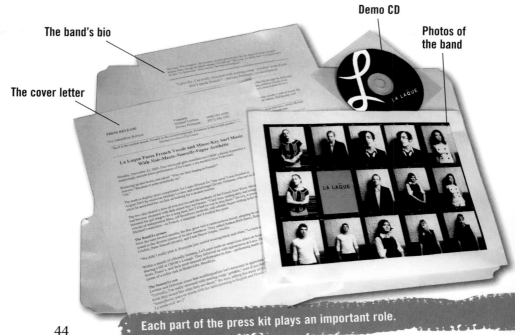

The band's bio

Demo CD

Photos of the band

The cover letter

Each part of the press kit plays an important role.

WHAT NEXT?

Say you've dropped off your press kit and cover letter at the club. Your work is not over yet. Bookers almost never call anyone back. They are so busy that they usually just wait for the bands to call them. Wait a week, and then call and tell them you dropped off a press kit a week ago. Ask if they have listened to your demo. Be polite. Do not annoy the booker, but do keep calling! It's a good idea to call once every few weeks to see if the booker has listened to your music. Sometimes you can book a show just by being persistent.

This approach is the way most bands get their first booking. Don't get discouraged if it takes a while to get your first show. Keep at it. One day, all of the hard work will pay off. You may get a call from a booker saying, "Okay, want to play Tuesday night, June 15, at 9 p.m.?" Given how hard it is to get booked, you immediately say, "We'll be there!"

Another way to get a show is to be asked by another band to be its opening act. An opening act goes on before a featured band to get the crowd excited. This is how La Laque got its first show.

A friend of mine had a band that had been playing shows in New York City for a long time. I told him about La Laque and asked if we could open for his band sometime. The next time he booked a show, he told the booker about La Laque. The booker called me and told us we would be the opening act. It was amazing. So, the lesson is that sometimes you can speed things up if you know the right people.

It's not really that important how you get your first show as long as you get it. Once you get your first show, there's only one thing left to do—and that's rock and roll!

CHAPTER 4
THE FIRST SHOW

It was really exciting when we got our first show. We felt like we had finally made it, and we hadn't even played for anyone yet. Little did we know how much work lay ahead. First, we had to figure out how to **lure** a crowd. Remember, the booker's job is to hire bands that bring people to the club. If you attract a lot of fans, the booker will ask you to play again. If no one comes to hear you play, the booker won't invite you back, ever.

Here's what we did to bring out a crowd to our first show. We called our friends to ask them to come to the show. Then, we sent out an e-mail reminder to all our friends a couple of days before the show. We also made posters to advertise our show. Posters are a great way to spread the news about your band. "Every time I tell someone about La Laque, they've already heard of us," says Leah, who designs our posters. "They say, 'I've seen the posters with that girl singer, right?' It's cool that people remember our posters."

Lots of bands print posters and fliers on their computers or at the copy center, while others draw them by hand. One cool poster tacked up in the perfect spot can be seen by a lot of people. If you hang a poster at a school or in a store, be sure to ask permission, though.

Another good way to publicize your show is to get a local newspaper or magazine to write about you. Lots of local magazines list shows that are happening at any given time. Remember your press kit? Send it to local newspapers, local magazines, and local radio stations. A magazine writer might write about your band or a newspaper reporter might come to see you and give you a review. People who read the review may get interested and attend your next show. Maybe you'll get really lucky and a DJ will play one of your songs on the radio.

Now that you have your friends going to the big show, you need to make sure you have all the equipment that you'll need. Besides instruments, you will need amplifiers for all of your instruments—except the drums. Amplifiers make the music loud enough for the audience to hear, but the drums are loud enough on their own. You will also need microphones for your lead singer and any backup singers in your band.

If you don't have everything you need, you may be able to borrow equipment from another band. Most bands will **cooperate** if they have something you need. Just ask the club for the other bands' phone numbers and call them if you need to borrow any equipment.

Once you have figured out the equipment you will need, you have to arrange to get it to the show. Load it all into a car or truck. Be sure to **cooperate** on loading the equipment into a car or truck. It can cause **conflicts** if someone has to do it alone. For example, in our band, Pete drives our equipment to every show because he's the only one with a car. However, Devery always helps out. As she says, "Don't you dare tell me I'm not strong enough to carry an amp. I even carry amps when I wear high heels!"

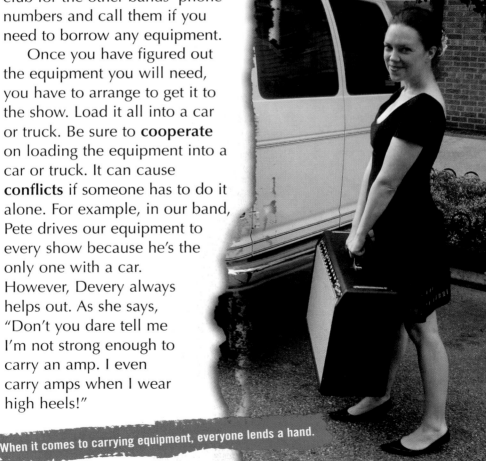

When it comes to carrying equipment, everyone lends a hand.

TESTING, ONE, TWO, THREE

Once a band gets its equipment to the club and sets up, it's time for a sound check. A sound check is when the band plays a few songs to make sure it sounds right onstage. Most clubs hire someone to control the sound. It's good to ask the booker when the sound check will be, and be sure to get to the club on time.

"I always want to have a sound check," says Devery. "Our band is loud and I sing very quietly. So, sometimes I can't tell if I'm singing in tune or not. At a sound check, I can tell the sound person to turn up my voice in the monitors." Monitors are big speakers in front of the band that help the musicians hear what they are playing. After a sound check, you wait for your friends to show up. Once the place fills up, it's time to go on!

One drawback about live shows is that things can sometimes go wrong. Equipment can break, someone can make a mistake and you have to start a song over. No matter what happens, keep your cool. It's awful to see a band panic onstage. Panicking doesn't help. Even if you are scared, you don't want the audience to know that.

Even the coolest people can lose control. For example, Devery hates feedback. Feedback is that high whiny sound that hurts your eardrums. "I know it's stupid, but feedback makes me want to cry," explains Devery. Once, at a club, the monitors were feeding back the whole show. Devery was about to cry. To stop herself from crying onstage, she yelled at the sound person! She felt sorry about it later, but at the time she was really on edge.

I remember how nervous we were before our first show. From the minute we woke up that morning, all we could think about was the fact that we would be playing in front of a live audience that night. We knew that we had spent hours and hours practicing for this moment. Still, we couldn't help but feel nervous.

LIVE WIRE!

As it turned out, our first show didn't go very well. The sound person didn't show up until a few minutes before we went on, so we didn't even get a sound check. "I was scared to death," Devery said. "It was our first show and everything was going wrong."

A hundred of our friends came, so the club was completely full. It was really scary to play in front of so many people. We started playing in **unison**, and it was going okay. We were doing fine. Then, Erin's amplifier broke. No one could hear the violin. We didn't know what to do, so we just kept playing. "I wasn't too upset about people not being able to hear me," Erin said. "I mostly felt guilty because I thought I had ruined the show."

"It wasn't so bad," Leah says. "It was okay because we were able to keep playing. It's much worse when Michael breaks a string. When that happens, we have to stop playing until he fixes it. That's horrible. I hate just standing onstage doing nothing. It's embarrassing."

Even though there are no **barriers** to the things that can go wrong during a live show, it's still the best part of being in a band. We all love being onstage in front of people.

"Playing onstage is the greatest," Pete says. "There's nothing more fun."

"I love looking into the audience while we play," Erin says. "I can see people dancing or smiling or bobbing their heads. The more the audience moves, the harder we rock."

Personally, I'm usually disappointed by shows. It's probably because I'm a perfectionist, so I always feel like we could have played better. Everyone comes up after the show and tells us how good we sounded, but I still can't tell if they're honest or just being nice. I am a lot harder on the band than the audience is.

La Laque onstage

Our best show ever was in Brooklyn, New York, at a party called Rock and Roller-skate. The show was at a skating rink. We played in a cage in the middle of the rink while the crowd roller-skated around us! Devery jumped on the walls of the cage and hung on while she sang. "The cage wasn't to keep the rollerskaters out," Pete says. "The cage was a **barrier** to keep Devery in!" Another fun show was a rooftop party in New York City. We had the whole cityscape behind us and the stars above us. It was an awesome show.

Those shows were great. It is so much fun playing for crowds of **animated** friends. We also have fun at shows where we play for a lot of people we don't know. Our main goal is to attract new fans. "I love it when we have to convince the crowd that we're good," Devery says.

I agree with Devery. Our friends already like us, and they've been following us since the beginning. It's more of a challenge when you are playing for people who have never heard of you.

"We're lucky," Brad says, "Everyone pays attention to us as soon as they see Devery. She really grabs the audience's attention."

GETTING PAID!

Live bands are a good way for clubs to draw big crowds. At most clubs, people have to pay to get in. The money collected at the door is called the "door." If you are going to play at a club, find out *ahead of time* from the **management** how much of the door your band can expect. Some clubs give the band all the money from the door, while other clubs only give the band part of the door and keep the rest to cover expenses.

One time, a club's manager told us we would get the whole door, but when the manager saw how many people we brought, he changed his mind. It became a **conflict**. He hadn't **calculated** on so many people coming to see us. The club's management tried to give us half of what we had agreed on, but we were firm. We argued with him until he gave us our money.

If you bring a lot of people to a club, there shouldn't be any **obstacles** to playing there again. Once the booker knows you and trusts that you will bring a crowd, he or she will give you another show. The best time slots are Friday and Saturday nights. If you keep playing shows that attract big crowds, the booker may give you those better time slots.

Imagine being so popular that one night in one city isn't enough. What if people all over the country will want to see you play? The crowds can't all come to your city, so you'll have to go to them.

CHAPTER 5
ROCK AROUND THE WORLD

After a band has played some shows around town, what's next? The band members have to be **industrious**. They have to make it their business to figure out how to get more people to hear their music. There are two great ways to do this: going online and going on tour.

What's the easiest way for fans to hear a band's music and find out when they are playing? Lots of music lovers look at band Web sites. One of the **obstacles** for a band is that Web sites are expensive to build and maintain. A band usually has to pay extra for a Web designer to create its site, too. We were lucky because Leah designs posters *and* Web sites! However, there are lots of people who know how to design Web sites. You can look online for Web designers. Another good way is to pick a band Web site you like and find out who designed it. Usually, the name of the designer will be at the bottom of the Web site.

Bands can make back some of their Web site costs by selling CDs and T-shirts on their Web site. T-shirts make money and they also help advertise the band. Plus, it's just cool to see people wearing your band's name on a T-shirt. Some bands make T-shirts themselves and some pay to have them made. Bands also make buttons and stickers to put up everywhere.

One other idea is that a band's Web site should have songs that fans can download. That way, fans can play the songs for themselves and their friends. The more fans listen to your music, the better they will know your sound. People will come to the band's shows already knowing the words to the band's songs. That makes for an **animated** crowd!

ALL ABOARD!

Touring can be really fun. Going on tour may mean playing clubs in nearby cities and towns, or it may mean playing clubs across the United States. The band spends every night playing music in another town and meeting all kinds of interesting people. Of course, a tour can be terrible if no one attends the shows. One goal of touring is to build your band's fan base. Another goal of touring is to make money, so if no one attends the shows, a tour can actually cost a band money. It's expensive to drive to the shows and stay in hotels.

When a band goes on its first tour, it can be hard to draw fans. Think about it. If it's your first time in a city, how could anybody have heard about you? For this reason, most new bands tour as an opening act. Usually, a lot of people come out to see the headliner. The headliner is the bigger, more famous band that plays last. The main benefit of being an opening act is that you get to play in front of a lot of people who may not have heard about you otherwise. It is a great way to get people to know your band and your music.

Touring is expensive for headliners *and* opening acts. The cost can be a big **obstacle**. Bands have to consider how expensive it is to go on tour. Gas is expensive. Motel rooms are even more expensive! I know all of this because La Laque recently went on tour.

We went on a small tour up and down the East Coast. We opened for a friend's band called Careful. Touring with a more experienced band helped us a lot. If you're on tour with a band that's already famous, you don't have to worry about drawing a crowd. Experienced bands are always looking for new bands to tour with. They can help share expenses, for example. Lots of successful bands keep track of who the cool new bands are.

Once you've gone on tour, you'll have lots of crazy tour stories to tell. "Once, a couple in Connecticut saw us play," says Brad. "They asked if we could stay in town another day and play at their wedding. We stayed in town and played in a room full of flower bouquets to a crowd of people in tuxedos! It was so weird."

La Laque's last tour was successful. We played in front of some big crowds. A lot of people who saw us play asked where they could find more information about our band. We also learned a lot from the headliner. Anytime we had questions about touring, the members of the headliner took the time to explain things to us. After such a great experience, we can't wait to go on tour again.

Ready to roll? Pete and Brad are set for another road trip.

CHAPTER 6
RECORD TIME

Playing live and going on tour are the main goals of some bands. Other bands don't like touring as much. These bands are more interested in recording their music. La Laque has **lofty** goals. We want to do both! Unfortunately, just like playing in clubs, there can be many **barriers** to making a quality CD. As you'll find out, some of the issues have to do with money.

Some bands use a producer to help them record their CD. A producer helps a band create the best CD it possibly can. The producer and the band should work together during the recording sessions. How far should the microphone be from the singer's mouth? How loud should the guitar be compared to the drums? Should the band try the song again or is that take good enough? With a producer, a band doesn't have to think about everything alone.

Unfortunately, most new bands don't have enough money to pay a professional producer. That's okay because a band *can* record a CD all by itself. Remember how I said a band can record a demo? A band can use the same equipment to record a CD—it just takes a lot longer to do ten songs instead of two. Then, the band can try to sell it to a record company. If the band records itself, it can send the recording to different record companies. If a company likes the music, it may buy the CD, make copies, and sell them in stores—if you're lucky.

If a record company pays for you to record the CD in the first place, the record company owns the rights to the CD. That can be bad. A band could record a great CD and the company says, "We don't like it. We won't release it." There's not much the band can do about it. The CD belongs to the company.

FINDING THE RIGHT RECORD LABEL

Before you think about recording and sending your music to record companies, you should know how record companies work. Record companies are also called record labels. Some famous labels are Columbia, Bad Boy, and SST. There are different kinds of record labels. For example, some companies record hip-hop, others record rock, and others record country. It is important to locate the right kinds of labels for your music. The company and its bands have to work in **harmony**—they have to have the same goals.

A label's distribution is very important. The distribution is how many copies of a CD a record label makes and where it sends them. Labels vary widely. Some labels print 1,000 copies of a CD. Some print 1,000,000. Some labels only put copies of their CDs in local stores in their city. Other labels send copies to every record store in the world. Some small labels are happy if their band sells 20,000 CDs. Major labels are disappointed if a band doesn't sell 500,000 CDs! The band must see eye to eye with the record label about distribution.

All bands want to sell lots of CDs, and they are willing to do whatever it takes to meet this goal. Sometimes meeting this goal means that a band has to deliberately change its sound to sell more CDs. It may need to write catchier songs and have lots of hit songs on the radio. Some bands don't want to change their sound, even if it means giving up the idea of selling more CDs. For bands like this, it's important that they find a record label that is **cooperative** about giving them total control over their music.

Another important issue is how much money a record label will pay you. Some labels pay a lot of money to a band when it signs a recording contract. Others can barely afford to pay for a band to record its songs.

You might think all rock stars are rich, but most of them are not. The bands playing in stadiums are rich, but the members of lots of great bands with thousands of fans still work regular jobs.

La Laque hasn't signed a recording contract…yet. We *are* almost finished recording our first two songs. We're recording them with a famous musician as our producer. This musician saw us at one of our shows. He introduced himself and said he wanted to produce us for free in his studio. We couldn't believe our luck.

Practice makes perfect. Devery records at the studio.

Now, our goal is to sign a recording contract with a good, small label. We probably won't make much money. We just want to have a CD out. We don't have **lofty** dreams of selling millions of CDs, but we do hope to sell thousands!

Our plan is to finish these two songs. We'll send them out to labels we like and try to get money to record an entire CD. One label already wants to put out our first two songs as a CD single. That's a CD with only two songs on it. The benefit of this label is that it has good distribution. It will send the single to radio stations all over the United States as well as all over Europe and Japan. Maybe we will have an entire CD in stores by the time this book is printed.

IN SESSION

Recording isn't easy. It has led to some **conflicts** among our band members. As I said before, I'm a perfectionist. "I used to hate recording because Michael made me sing everything a million times," says Devery. "Now, I see that it's good to keep trying until it's perfect. It's horrible to listen to your recording and hear mistakes over and over!"

Erin says, "In live shows, people don't hear your mistakes. But on recordings, they can hear everything!"

However, Leah says, "Michael goes too far. He hears mistakes even when they're not there! And besides, mistakes aren't so bad. It's more raw if it has mistakes!"

Of course, I disagree with Leah. Still, plenty of musicians agree that it ruins the music if the recording sounds too perfect. Pete agrees with Leah. "Michael makes the recordings harder than they have to be," Pete says. "He always wants to add things we don't do live."

Pete is right about that. What I like best about recording is that you can add extra sounds. I add cellos and violas and lots of extra guitars. Sometimes Devery sings **harmony** with herself. On the recording, we'll sound like a band of ten people instead of just six.

The most important advice is to go into the studio knowing what you're doing. You should have thoroughly practiced every song *before* you get to the studio. Recording time is not the time to be learning the music. You don't want to waste that expensive time.

Recording can be very important, but not for every band. Some bands only care about being good in live performances, while other bands are more interested in making good recordings. I want La Laque to be great at both. I definitely want the CDs to be different from our live show. I think it's boring when a live band sounds just like its CD.

I hope this book helps you know what it is like trying to achieve rock stardom. I have tried to tell you about some of the issues that have to be faced based on my own experiences with La Laque. Here are a few more things to remember.

First of all, remember that most bands never become rich and famous. Some of the best bands keep playing for years before anyone knows who they are. There are amazing bands that have never had a hit. On the other hand, some terrible bands also become very popular. Some very popular bands still never make much money. Some bands are famous, but only people over 40 years old know who they are. Then, there are even bands that have only 1,000 fans, but these fans follow them all over the place!

WHAT ARE YOU WAITING FOR?

If you're going to be in a band, you've got to do it because you love it. You should play music because it makes you happy. If you're only in a band for the **lofty** goal of seeking money or fame, you're likely to be disappointed.

As you have read here, being in a band isn't always fun. It takes a great deal of hard work. You don't always make money, and most bands aren't famous. You have to go through all of the work just because you love to play.

Even if your dream comes true and you become famous, your situation may change. You might have people to carry your equipment and lots of fans at your shows yet still worry that your new songs aren't good enough. Your record company could change its focus or your fans could abandon you. Those kinds of worries cause a lot of stress and fighting. That's why so many bands break up. Think about the Beatles. They were the most famous band the world had ever seen, yet the Beatles didn't even last 10 years.

Of course, I'm not trying to tell you that you should give up on your dream. I haven't given up my dream. I know it's going to be a long, hard adventure having a band. It is a huge challenge. There will be lots of **obstacles**. Sometimes there will be **conflicts** between band members. I also know it's what I want to do more than anything else in the world.

Devery says, "Now that I've had a band, I can't go back to living without it."

"There will never be a time in my life when I don't play music," Leah says.

"Even if I have to work in an office during the week and rock on the weekends, I'll do it," Brad says.

Now that you know what it's like being in a band, I hope you think it's pretty cool. Are you ready to rock? Then, rock on!

The band relaxes together between shows.

GLOSSARY

abruptly suddenly, unexpectedly, or without warning

accidental happening by chance, not planned. An **accident** is something that was not expected to happen.

agreement the condition of having the same opinion or of being alike or similar

animated full of liveliness

barriers things that separate or keep one place separate from another

calculated planned or done on purpose

chaos great disorder and confusion. **Chaotic** means lacking order.

commercials paid advertisements that are shown on a TV or played on a radio

conflicts struggles or disagreements

cooperative willing to work with others. To **cooperate** means to work together with others.

deliberately carefully thought out or planned

disastrous causing much damage or suffering. **Disasters** are happenings that cause much damage or suffering.

distorted twisted out of its usual shape or changed in order to give a false idea. If there is **distortion**, there is fuzziness.

enthusiasm strong liking or interest; eagerness. Something done with great interest is done **enthusiastically**.

exquisite very beautiful and delicate

glamorous full of fascinating charm, attraction, and beauty

harmony a combination of musical sounds that are sung or played together. To **harmonize** means to sing or play together.

humiliation the feeling of being ashamed or embarrassed. If someone's pride is taken away, he or she feels **humiliated**.

industrious hardworking

intrigued very interested or fascinated by something or someone. If someone or something is **intriguing**, that person or thing is fascinating.

lofty superior

lure to persuade someone to go somewhere or do something by tempting the person

management the organization in control of a business. **Managers** are the people who direct and control a business.

obstacles people or things that prevent progress

overcrowded full of too many people or things

pose to put one's body into a position. **Posing** is getting into a certain position.

probably very likely to happen. **Probability** means good chance or without much doubt.

realistic seeing things as they really are; practical. **Reality** is the condition of being real.

tormented caused pain to somebody or something

transforming changing the form or looks of someone or something. When the look of someone or something is changed, it is **transformed**.

uncertainty lack of sureness, doubt

unison two or more notes or parts that are sung or said together

INDEX